MARTIN LUTHER KING JR.

KRISTEN SUSIENKA

PowerKiDS press™

New York

Published in 2020 by The Rosen Publishing Group, Inc.
29 East 21st Street, New York, NY 10010

First Edition

Editor: Kristen Susienka
Book Design: Michael Flynn

Photo Credits: Cover, p. 1 Martin Mills/Archive Photos/Getty Images; series background Kharchenko Rusian/Shutterstock.com; p. 5 Reg Lancaster/Hulton Archive/Getty Images; pp. 7, 13, 15, 19 Bettmann/Getty Images; p. 9 Michael Ochs Archives/Getty Images; p. 11 (map) pingebat/Shutterstock.com; p. 11 (paper texture) Color Symphony/Shutterstock.com; p. 11 (house) Mccallk69/Shutterstock.com; p. 17 -/AFP/Getty Images; p. 21 kropic1/Shutterstock.com.

Library of Congress Cataloging-in-Publication Data

Names: Susienka, Kristen, author.
Title: Martin Luther King Jr. / Kristen Susienka.
Description: New York : PowerKids Press, 2020. | Series: African American
   leaders of courage | Includes index.
Identifiers: LCCN 2019012228| ISBN 9781725308473 (pbk.) | ISBN 9781725308480
   (library bound) | ISBN 9781725308466 (6 pack)
Subjects: LCSH: King, Martin Luther, Jr., 1929-1968–Juvenile literature. |
   African Americans–Biography–Juvenile literature. | Civil rights
   workers–United States–Biography–Juvenile literature. | African
   Americans–Civil rights–History–20th century–Juvenile literature. |
   Civil rights movements–United States–History–20th century–Juvenile
   literature.
Classification: LCC E185.97.K5 S87 2020 | DDC 323.092 [B] –dc23
LC record available at https://lccn.loc.gov/2019012228

CONTENTS

Working for Justice

Martin Luther King Jr. was a very important leader in the **civil rights movement** of the 1950s and 1960s. He believed in **justice** for everyone and standing up for what's right. He believed in change through peaceful means and showing kindness to others.

Growing Up in the South

Martin Luther King Jr. was born in 1929. He and his family lived in Atlanta, Georgia. His father was a preacher, or religious leader. **Segregation** was a part of life in the South. Martin would help change that.

FOR
COLORED
ONLY

Getting an Education

Martin loved learning and did well in school and college. He went to a **seminary** school in 1948. In the mid-1950s, he earned a **doctorate** from a school in Boston, Massachusetts. He married Coretta Scott in 1953.

9

Moving to Montgomery

In 1954, Martin and Coretta moved to Montgomery, Alabama. Martin became a preacher like his father. Montgomery was a very segregated city. Blacks and whites couldn't go to school or ride buses together. The black community wanted that to change.

UNITED STATES OF AMERICA

Boycotts

In December 1955, a woman named Rosa Parks refused to give her seat on a Montgomery bus to a white man. She was arrested. Martin led a group of African Americans who started a bus **boycott** that lasted more than a year. After this, bus segregation ended.

MARX
GOOD OR YOUR DIAL

Answering with Peace

Martin Luther King Jr. became the leader of the nationwide movement to end segregation. Many people helped him, and many people hurt him. It wasn't easy. He planned and led peaceful marches and other actions, even though he was arrested. Answering with peace could lead to change.

15

March on Washington

In August 1963, Martin and thousands of others marched in Washington, D.C., calling for change. He gave a powerful speech now often called "I Have a Dream." It painted a picture of a United States in which people were equal.

Success and Sadness

In 1964, Martin won the Nobel Peace Prize. The same year, Congress passed the Civil Rights Act. The act ended segregation by law in public places. Other successes followed, including the Voting Rights Act of 1965. However, in April 1968, Martin was **assassinated**.

Martin Lives On

The spirit of Martin Luther King Jr. lives on today. He's remembered every January on Martin Luther King Jr. Day. A statue in his honor stands in Washington, D.C. His family and others continue working for justice and equality everywhere.

THE LIFE OF MARTIN LUTHER KING JR.

1929	Martin Luther King Jr. is born.
1953	Martin earns a doctorate and marries Coretta Scott.
1955	Martin leads the Montgomery bus boycott.
1964	Martin delivers his "I Have a Dream" speech and the Civil Rights Act is passed.
1968	Martin is assassinated.

GLOSSARY

assassinate: To kill someone, especially a public figure.

boycott: A refusal to buy, use, or take part in something.

civil rights movement: A time period in U.S. history starting in the 1950s in which African Americans fought for equal civil rights, or the freedoms granted to us by law.

doctorate: The highest degree given by a university.

justice: Fair treatment.

segregation: The separation of people based on race, class, or ethnicity.

seminary: A school for religious leaders.

INDEX

WEBSITES

Due to the changing nature of Internet links, PowerKids Press has developed an online list of websites related to the subject of this book. This site is updated regularly. Please use this link to access the list: www.powerkidslinks.com/AALC/king